M O N E Y
...and how it multiplies!

A Practical Guide for Effective Money Management

Dr. Mia Y. Merritt

Copyright 2013
by Mia Y. Merritt, Ed.D
MONEY and how it multiplies WORKBOOK

All rights reserved. No part of this book
may be reproduced in any form without permission
in writing from the author or publisher.

ISBN #9780983583011

Other Books by Mia Y. Merritt:
Prosperity is Your Birthright!
Prosperity is Your Birthright Workbook
Destined for Great Things!
Destined for Great Things Workbook
Words of Inspiration
Life After High School
Life After High School Workbook
The Road the Inner Joy & Peace
Releasing Emotional Baggage
Money & How it Multiplies

Library of Congress Cataloging
in-Publication Data

Merritt, Mia

First Printing 2013
Printed in the U.S.A.

ABOUT THIS WORKBOOK

Hello my friend,

I'm so excited for you because you are on your way to effective financial literacy, and with a little discipline and commitment, you will find yourself in financial freedom! Before you continue turning the pages of this workbook, make sure that you have read and are familiar with the information in the book, *Money... and How it Multiplies*. This book was developed to help you retain and apply what you have learned about money management, your Credit Report, retirement, taxes, buying your first home, and a whole lot more!

The activities in this workbook are directly correlated to the chapters in the book. It would be of great benefit to you if you completed this workbook with the book by your side. After completing the exercises in this workbook, you will be able to know, recognize, apply, understand, and do the following:

- Apply basic money management strategies that will keep you out of debt
- Create a Spending Plan that will put you on the path to financial freedom
- Develop a budget that will assist you in reaching your financial goals
- Plan your financial future with beneficial information on investing and saving
- Understand the valuable reasons for saving for retirement early
- Learn how to keep your Credit Report in good standing
- Understand the advantages and disadvantages of credit card use
- Distinguish between 401Ks, 403Bs & Roth IRAs
- Differentiate between the different types of insurance
- Learn everything you need to know about the home buying process

This workbook is an interactive, hands-on, thought-provoking guide about effective money management! It is designed to help you understand how money works and how to make it work for you. You are at a great advantage by completing the exercises in this book. After completing them, you will be on the path to financial freedom! Are you ready? Are you Set? Then, let's go.

Turn the Page

CONTENTS

About This Workbook iii

Chapter 1: How Money Works 1

Chapter 2: Create Your Spending Plan 5

Chapter 3: Your Credit Report 9

Chapter 4: Become Financially Literate 15

Chapter 5: Plan Your Future 21

Chapter 6: Understand Your Taxes 25

Chapter 7: Buying Your First Home 37

About the Author 72

~ 1 ~

 ## How Money Works

*Money is like a sixth sense - and you can't make use
of the other five without it.*
~William Somerset Maugham

1. The way you handle money will eventually affect major financial purchases of your life such as the purchase of:

    i. _____

    ii. _____

    iii. _____

2. Name two accounts that banks sometimes offer for no monthly fee.

    i. _____

    ii. _____

3. Name two companies that sell checkbooks at discounted prices.

    i. _____

    ii. _____

4. The key to becoming wealthy is not how much money you make, but how much of it you _____

5. When the amount you spend is larger than the amount you make, then the only option you have is to do what? _____

6. Why is it important to save a set amount of every dollar you earn? _____
_____
_____

7. What is the purpose of keeping a balanced checkbook? _____
_____
_____

8. List some things that can happen when your debt gets too out-of-control.

      i. _____

      ii. _____

      iii. _____

9. The amount of money you bring home each month is referred to as what kind of income? _____.

10. What is the benefit of checking your bank account online frequently? _____
_____
_____

11. Why should you review the amount of money you bring home each month with the amount you spend each month? _____
_____

12. Why is it a good idea to check your credit report every six to twelve months? _____
_____
_____

Keeping your checkbook balanced is fundamental to financial literacy and essential to financial responsibility.

13. Name at least six things that you can do to keep your credit record in good standing.

    i. _____

How does this benefit your credit record? _____

    ii. _____

How does this benefit your credit record? _____

    iii. _____

How does this benefit your credit record? _____

    iv. _____

How does this benefit your credit record? _____

    v. _____

How does this benefit your credit record? _____

    vi. _____

How does this benefit your credit record? _____

14. A budget is also called a _____ plan.

15. What is the benefit in going AUTOMATIC? _____
_____
_____

16. Name some accounts that you can set up to go automatic:

    i. _____
    ii. _____
    iii. _____
    iv. _____

FINANCIAL TIPS TO REMEMBER:

- ✓ You must make it an automatic habit of saving a portion of every dollar you earn.

- ✓ As you write checks, make sure that you keep your checkbook balanced to ensure that the money to cover each check written is available.

- ✓ If you are spending more than you are earning, it is time to review your spending habits. When the expenditures are larger than the income, you have one only option: cut your expenses.

- ✓ Paying back your debts in a timely manner helps you to maintain a good credit history and will allow you to get better rates on major purchases.

- ✓ If you have allowed your credit to go bad, you can still build it back up again. Don't get discouraged.

~ 2 ~

Create Your Spending Plan

*Too many people spend money they haven't earned,
to buy things they don't want, to impress people they don't like.*
~Will Smith

1. What is the benefit of sticking to a spending plan? _____
   _____
   _____

2. When creating a spending plan, what are the top five expenditures to consider?

   i. _____
   ii. _____
   iii. _____
   iv. _____
   v. _____

3. In your own words, what is an Emergency Fund? _____
   _____
   _____
   _____

4. If you currently to not have an Emergency Fund, what is the first thing you should do?
   _____

5. According to what you have learned, what is the best way to get started on your Emergency Fund? _____

6. An ideal Emergency Fund amount should have how many months of household expenses in it? _____

7. In starting an Emergency Fund, the first thing you need to know is how much money you spend each month. On the lines below, fill in the spaces that represent your top ten monthly bills, then add them up at bottom:

BILL	AMOUNT
TOTTAL MONTHLY EXPENSES →	

8. Based on the figure you have come up with, what is the amount of money you need saved for a three month Emergency Fund? _____

9. How much would you need for a six-month Emergency Fund? _____ (multiply by 2)

10. In order to determine if you are in debt, the first thing you should do is what? _____

_____

_____

11. What typically keeps most people in debt? _____

_____

12. Name at least two things that one should do to keep their Emergency Fund growing.

    I. _____

    II. _____

13. What are some of the quickest ways to accumulate debt? _____

_____

_____

14. What are some questions that you should ask yourself before you buy something that tickles your fancy, but is a non-essential?

    I. _____

    II. _____

    III. _____

    IV. _____

Being financial responsible gives you peace of mind in knowing that there is money in savings when you need it. Peace of mind makes for a happy camper!

15. In Chapter two of your book, 'Money and How it Multiplies', there were 15 things listed that make your credit go bad. On the lines below, list at least ten of those 15 things listed.

THINGS THAT CAN MAKE MY CREDIT GO BAD:

I. _____

II. _____

III. _____

IV. _____

V. _____

VI. _____

VII. _____

VIII. _____

IX. _____

X. _____

FINANCIAL TIPS TO REMEMBER:

- Like every other recurring item in your budget, the Emergency Fund is something you put money into each month until you reach your desired goal.

- If you currently do not have an Emergency Fund or find it difficult to save, the key is to start small. Even if you only start with $10.00 in the beginning, at least you have taken the initiative to start.

- If you keep your standard of living *below* what you earn, you will not have to cut back to save money, instead, you will have excess cash flow because you will earn more than you need to live on.

~ 3 ~

Your Credit Report

A person's credit report is one of the most important tools consumers can use to maintain their financial security and credit rating, but for so long many did not know how to obtain one, or what to do with the information it provided.
~Ruben Hinojosa

1. Based upon what you have learned, what is credit? _____
   _____
   _____

2. What is the main factor for a lender to determine your ability to pay back a loan? _____
   _____
   _____

3. Name two other factors that a creditor will consider before giving you a loan?

   I. _____

   II. _____

4. In your own words, what is an Annual Percentage Rate? _____
   _____
   _____

5. What is the first thing a lender looks at when you apply for credit? _____
   _____

6. In your own words, what is a Credit Report? _____
   _____
   _____

7. Your Credit Report is maintained by companies called what? _____

8. What is the role of lenders concerning your payment history to them after they extend credit to you? _____
   _____
   _____

9. What kinds of information do lenders report after they extend credit to you?

   I. _____

   II. _____

   III. _____

   IV. _____

   V. _____

10. Name some public financial records that may also appear on your Credit Report?

   I. _____

   II. _____

   III. _____

   IV. _____

   V. _____

11. What is some personal information that does not appear on your Credit Report?

  I. _____

  II. _____

  III. _____

  IV. _____

  V. _____

12. What is a credit bureau? _____
_____
_____

13. Name the three top credit bureaus in the United States:

  I. _____

  II. _____

  III. _____

14. Why is your credit score important?
_____
_____

15. If your credit score is bad, a lender may still extend credit to you, but what is the downside to this? _____
_____
_____

16. What ultimately makes the difference in your monthly payment? _____

17. What is a F.I.C.O. Score? _____
    _____
    _____

18. What is the benefit in having a high FICO (credit) score: _____
    _____
    _____

19. A FICO score takes into account a lot of different information from your Credit Report, but it is not all weighted equally. Name the five areas and percentages that make up a FICO score.

    I. _____ percentage: _____

    II. _____ percentage: _____

    III. _____ percentage: _____

    IV. _____ percentage: _____

    V. _____ percentage: _____

20. Notes left on your credit reports are usually indicated by codes indicated by **R1 to R9**. The "R" means that it is a "revolving" account. An R1 means that the account is a revolving account in good standing. An R9 means a revolving account in very poor standing. R1s and R9s are two extremes of the many account classifications that your creditors can add to your Credit Report. In the box below, complete the table with the appropriate R score.

R	REVOLVING
	30+ days past due
	90+ days past due
	Little or no credit history
	120+ days past the due date
	Chapter 13 of the Bankruptcy Code.
	Charge off to bad debt
	Repossession
	Paid as agreed
	This rating does not exist
	60+ days past due

21. On the average, how long does derogatory information remain on your credit report? _____

22. How often should you check your credit report? _____

23. What is the best method of obtaining a copy of your credit report? _____
_____

24. What is an alternate way of obtaining your credit report? _____

25. What are some ways in which you may obtain a free copy of your credit report? _____
_____
_____

FINANCIAL TIPS TO REMEMBER:

- Your Credit Report is the first thing that lenders look at when you apply for a credit card or want to make a major purchase.

- Lenders offer better terms and lower interest rates to consumers with good credit scores.

- Your Credit Report is a detailed record of your payment history with lenders and is an indicator that reflects how well or badly you manage your financial matters.

- A credit bureau is an agency that gathers information on how consumers use their credit and how they pay back what they borrowed.

- A FICO (Fair Isaac Corporation) Score is calculated based on the information contained in your Credit Report. The numbers are generated by a computer program that runs through your Report. It looks for patterns, characteristics, and red flags in your credit history.

~ 4 ~

Become Financially Literate

*Money is like a sixth sense and you can't make use of
the other five without it."*
~William Somerset Maugham

1. After you receive your paycheck, the IRS has already taken out taxes. What is the next thing you should do with at least 10 % of your money? _____

   _____

   _____

2. What are the three baskets a person should save money into?

   I. _____

   II. _____

   III. _____

3. What is the purpose of an Emergency Fund? _____

   _____

   _____

4. What is Emotional Spending? _____

   _____

5. Why should you never buy anything when you are desperate for it? _____
_____
_____

6. Are there some things that you purchase once a day, once a week, or once a month? If so list them and complete the activity below.

   A.

   _____ every _____ amount _____
   _____ every _____ amount _____
   _____ every _____ amount _____

   B. Multiply the amounts according to the frequency with which you purchase those items to come up with a yearly figure. (daily X 365, weekly X 52, monthly X 12)

   C. What is the figure? _____ _____ _____

   D. Take your yearly figure and write it here: _____ _____ _____

   E. If your calculations are correct, that's how much money you spend in one year on the item(s) above. Now ask yourself if this is something you can afford to give up. ___yes no___

   If yes, how will you divert that same amount of money to benefit you? In other words, what are you willing to do with that money when/if you stop spending it on the above items.

   _____
   _____

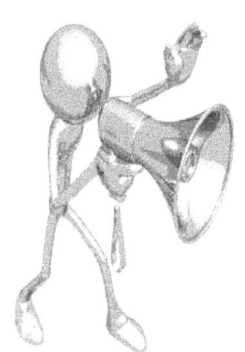

If you begin adding up all the small things you buy on a daily, weekly or monthly basis (coffee, bagel, cinnamon roll, nails, etc.), you will be SHOCKED how much all that adds up to!

7. When a consumer borrows money from a bank so that they can make a big purchase such as a house, car, or boat etc, that is called what? _____

8. Once a bank approves a loan that you have applied for, what do they do next? _____
   _____
   _____

9. If you discover that you are wasting a lot of money, would you be willing to curtail your spending? ___ yes ___ no. Why or why not? _____
   _____
   _____

TRUE OR FALSE?

10. It is fine to use credit cards for food and toiletries. _____
11. All credit cards have the same Annual Percentage Rate. _____
12. A credit card should ideally be used for things you can pay back in a month's time. _____
13. All credit cards have an annual fee. _____
14. Credit cards and debit cards are basically the same thing. _____
15. One should wait until they get older to save for retirement. _____
16. There are advantages and disadvantages to having credit cards. On the lines below list **three advantages** to having credit cards.

    I. _____
    II. _____
    III. _____

17. On the lines below, list **three disadvantages** to having credit cards.

    I. _____
    II. _____
    III. _____

18. On the lines below, list your **Credit Card Responsibilities** as a credit card holder.

   I. _____

   II. _____

   III. _____

   IV. _____

   V. _____

19. On the lines below, list some facts that you have learned about credit cards.

   I. _____

   II. _____

   III. _____

   IV. _____

   V. _____

20. What are the main components of the Credit Card Accountability, Responsibility and Disclosure Act of 2009?

   I. _____

   II. _____

   III. _____

   IV. _____

   V. _____

21. What is bankruptcy? _____
_____
_____

22. Most cases of bankruptcy are filed under what three codes?

    I. _____

    II. _____

    III. _____

23. This code is a formal declaration that you are willingly working with creditors so that they will eventually get their money from you, but at a slightly slower rate than they might have wanted. Under this code, by promising to pay off your debts, you are allowed to keep valuable personal items rather than turning them over to be sold. _____

24. Under this code, filing means that the business intends to continue operating while the bankruptcy court supervises the company's debt and contractual obligations. The court has the power to cancel all or some of the company's debts. The company can then make a fresh start without having the financial burden hanging over their head. _____

25. This filing means the selling off of your valuable assets in order to pay your debts. It does not mean that all of your debt is eliminated entirely. It means that all "unsecured" debt does not have to be paid back, but the "secured" debt must be dealt with in some kind of way_____

26. How does filing bankruptcy affect your credit? _____

_____

_____

If you keep your credit in good standing, you won't have to worry about bankruptcy. Remember to :

- ✓ Pay your bills on time
- ✓ Don't overextend yourself
- ✓ Don't use credit cards for non-essentials
- ✓ Save for retirement early
- ✓ Stay in the green

FINANCIAL TIPS TO REMEMBER:

- ✓ It is not about how much money you make, but much of your money you save or invest.

- ✓ Financing is a means of obtaining money, then paying the loan back in a specified time period for a set monthly amount.

- ✓ A credit card is a great financial backup and having the credit available for emergencies is definitely a life-saver, but your credit card should only be used for emergencies.

- ✓ The President Obama Administration passed *the Credit Card Accountability, Responsibility and Disclosure Act of 2009* for the purpose of attempting to remove those unfriendly terms that kept Americans in debt.

- ✓ Declaring yourself bankrupt can have disastrous long-term implications.

~ 5 ~

Plan for Your Future

If you fail to plan, you plan to fail.
~unknown

1. What is the benefit of setting financial goals and making plans for your financial future?

   _____

   _____

2. What are the two main things that determine the amount of federal income tax you pay?

   I. _____

   II. _____

3. For the current year, what percentage of your paycheck goes to FICA (Federal Insurance Contribution Act)? _____

4. For the current year, what percentage of your paycheck goes to Medicare? _____

5. The amount of money you have left after all of your deductions have been taken out is called your what? _____

6. What percentage of your income should you use to PAY YOURSELF FIRST? _____

7. What two accounts should you regularly put money into with the amount that you use to pay yourself first?

   I. _____

   _____

~ 21 ~

8. What is the purpose of the first account? _____

9. What is the purpose of the second account? _____

10. Once you secure your career, what is the first thing you should do? _____

_____

_____

11. What is the purpose of a Retirement Plan? _____

_____

12. What is the best way to put money into these accounts without having to think about doing it every time you get paid? _____

_____

13. What is the benefit in starting to save for retirement while you are young? _____

_____

_____

14. What does "tax deferred" mean? _____

15. When your retirement plan does not allow you to invest in stocks, but gives options of annuities, mutual funds and money market funds to invest in, this is which plan? _____

16. When your employer-sponsored retirement plan includes publicly traded securities and mutual funds, this is usually which plan? _____

17. With the Roth IRA, what is the maximum amount of money that can be contributed to the account each year? _____

18. A person over 50 may contribute up to how much into their IRA? _____

19. What is the age that you can make a withdrawal out of your retirement accounts without penalty? _____

20. At what age can you open an Roth IRA? _____

21. Name two popular Retirement Plans that companies, organizations, or businesses offer to their employees. _____ _____

22. What is an incentive that some organizations do for their employees when they contribute to their Retirement Plan? _____

23. If you leave a company that offered a Retirement Plan and begin working at a company that does not offer the plan, what can you do with the money you contributed from your previous employer? _____
_____

24. Look at the IRA characteristics below and put an **"R"** if the statement belongs to a **Roth** IRA and put a **"T"** if the statement refers to a **Traditional** IRA.

    _____ Individuals of all ages can open up a Roth

    _____ Pay a 10% penalty for early withdrawal

    _____ Must be at least 18 to open up a this account

    _____ You have to withdraw a minimum amount

    _____ Pay no taxes when you withdraw money at age 59 ½

    _____ Assets can be passed onto beneficiaries after death.

    _____ Contributions can be withdrawn at any time, tax free

    _____ There are no required minimum distributions

    _____ Pay taxes on the money you withdraw

    _____ Contributions ARE tax deductible

    _____ Contributions are NOT tax deductible

25. When the money you make from an initial investment is reinvested to make even more money than the initial investment that is called what? _____

> It is better to work hard and sacrifice while you are younger and relax when you are older verses relaxing when you are younger and having to work hard when you are older. "IF" you plan well, you will be so happy you did. There is nothing like having financial freedom when you really need it! Financial freedom gives peace and joy!

FINANCIAL TIPS TO REMEMBER:

➢ Research has shown that those who strategically plan for the future end up with more wealth than those who do not.

➢ The first 10% of what you make should always go to you. This is called PAYING YOURSELF FIRST:

➢ A primary distinction and excellent benefit of the 401k and 403b Plans is the fact that the money invested is tax deferred, meaning that the salary deferrals are pre-taxed until you reach the age of being able to withdraw it.

➢ The secret that makes the rich get richer is this: If you put your money in an investment that delivers a good return and then reinvest those earnings as you receive them, the snowball effect can be astounding over the long term.

~ 6 ~

Taxes & Insurance

The difference between death and taxes is death doesn't get worse every time Congress meets.
~Will Rogers

1. The biggest tax you pay to the government is what? _____

2. What is the name of the form that determines how much money will be taken out of your check when you are hired at a job? _____

3. How often does the company you work for pay federal withholding taxes to the government? _____

4. How does claiming more dependants on your W4 Form affect the money that you bring home?
_____
_____

5. How does claiming less dependants on your W4 Form affect the money that you bring home?
_____
_____

6. Why do some people have their federal withholding percentage set high? _____
_____
_____

7. What is FICA (*Federal Insurance Contributions Act*)? _____

   _____

   _____

8. What kinds of things does FICA pay for?

   I. _____

   II. _____

   III. _____

   IV. _____

   V. _____

9. What is the percentage of FICA that is taken out of everyone's paycheck? _____

10. Broken down, what is the individual percentage of social security and Medicare that makes the total FICA tax?

    SS: _____

    Medicare: _____

11. What kind of things do your income taxes pay for?

    I. _____

    II. _____

    III. _____

    IV. _____

    V. _____

12. What kinds of things do state taxes pay for?

   I. _____

   II. _____

   III. _____

   IV. _____

   V. _____

13. Your tax bracket depends upon two things: 1.) your taxable income and 2.) your filing status. What are the codes for the following tax brackets (1-5)?

   Single _____

   Married Filing Jointly _____

   Married Filing Separately _____

   Head of Household _____

   Qualifying Widow(er) _____

14. How many years should a person retain copies of their tax returns? _____

15. Do you have medical insurance?   ___ yes ___ no

16. If not, what will you do if you require medical attention? _____
_____
_____

17. How do you plan on getting medical insurance in the near future if you do not have any?
_____
_____

18. Do you have life insurance? ___yes ___ no

> If yes, do you know which of the two kinds it is (term or whole life)?
>
> ___yes ___ no

21. What is the difference between the two different kinds of life insurance?

_____

_____

22. Analyzing your personal situation, which type of insurance is best for you?

> ___ Whole Life Insurance
>
> ___ Term Life Insurance

23. Do you have enough life insurance to bury you and pay off all your debt? ___yes ___ no

PART B:

24. If you have credit cards, complete the exercises below. If not, skip the exercise.

List all your credit cards below:

CREDIT CARD	BALANCE OWED	CREDIT LIMIT	APR%	TARGET DATE TO PAY IT OFF

25. Based on the table above, how much money do you owe in credit card debt? $_____

In helping you to develop a Spending Plan, complete the following exercises:

26. My annual (gross) income is: _____ My net income (every paycheck) is _____. My federal withholding amount is _____. My FICA/Social Security amount is _____.

List all of your payroll deductions and amounts below:

DEDUCTION	AMOUNT PER PAYCHECK	TOTAL PER MONTH
Ex: Medical Ins.	$ 153.00	$306.00
United Way	$15.00	$30.00

27. According to your figures above, what is the total amount of your deductions including taxes per year? _____

28. Review all of your deductions above and see if there are any that you can cut out.

List them below:

ITEM	AMOUNT PER CHECK	AMOUNT SAVED PER YEAR

On the lines below, make a list all of your MONTHLY household expenses.

Example:	AMOUNT	TOTAL
Rent	$750.00	$750.00
Car Payment	$300.00	$300.00
	TOTTAL MONTHLY EXPENSES →	

29. I bring home this amount each month: _____.

   My total monthly expenses are: _____.

30. As I review my income and calculate my monthly expenses, I am (choose one):

   ___ in the green (positive) with _____ dollars left over each month.

   ___ in the red (negative) by _____ dollars each month.

31. If you have money left over each month, do you see where the extra money (surplus) goes?

   ___ yes   ___ no.   Explain on the lines below:

   _____

   _____

(The exercise on page 32 can help to reveal where the money goes.)

32. If you do not have money left over, what do you need to do to change this?

   _____

   _____

33. Based on what you have learned, where should your extra money be going?

   _____

   _____

Part C: FINANCIAL EXERCISE:
For one month, keep a record of everything you spend. Do this for 30 consecutive days. It is better to start on the first day of the month, however, if you start on April 15th, then you must review your findings on May 15th. This includes everything paid out of your net income (rent, car payment, utilities, clothes, food, etc.) This does not include deductions that are already taken out.

You are given extra lines for the days that you buy more than one or two things in a day. (You may buy a new shirt, then gas, a cup of coffee, then a meal at Red Lobster. You may then pick up a prescription at the local drug store – all in the same day. You must keep track of each of these things and put them in your log. Log everything you spend for one month. You will be surprised!

Date to begin: _____

DATE	STORE	PURCHASE	AMOUNT	TOTAL

DATE	STORE	PURCHASE	AMOUNT	TOTAL

FINANCIAL TIPS TO REMEMBER:

- Having a retirement account saves and protects you significantly from getting hit hard by taxes.

- FICA is an acronym that stands for *Federal Insurance Contributions Act* and is a tax is a percentage of money that is taken out of the paychecks of working individuals to pay Social Security Retirement and Medicare (Hospital Insurance) benefits to older Americans.

- Your tax bracket depends upon two things: 1.) your taxable income and 2.) your filing status.

- Your filing status is based upon your marital and family situation on the last day of the tax year.

- Make sure that you keep copies of your income tax returns for at least seven (ideally ten) years because you will need them for various things at various times.

It's time to take control of your finances and make your money work for you instead of you working for money.
It's TIME to WAKE UP!

Buying Your First Home!

I always thought a yard was three feet, then I started mowing the lawn.

~C.E. Cowman

1. What are some of the differences between home ownership and renting? _____

   i. _____

   ii. _____

   iii. _____

2. How soon in advance should you typically begin preparing for homeownership? _____
_____

3. What are the main three things that should be done BEFORE you begin the home-buying process?

   i. _____

   ii. _____

   iii. _____

4. What is the difference between getting pre-qualified and getting pre-approved?

_____

_____

_____

5. During the pre-approval process, you will need certain documents. List some of the documents that you will need when seeking to apply for a home loan.

   I. _____

   II. _____

   III. _____

   IV. _____

   V. _____

6. What is the primary thing that creditors look for when a client seeks to apply for a home loan?

_____

7. How soon after a client applies for a home loan should they receive the Good Faith Estimate?

_____

8. What is a GFE? _____

_____

_____

9. Why should you carefully review the GFE when you get it? _____

_____

_____

Lenders follow two rules of thumb to determine how much you can afford to pay. Your pre-approval may go through with certain "conditions." These conditions will need to be satisfied as soon as possible.

10. Your mortgage payment should not be more than _____% of your gross monthly income?

11. This is known as your what? _____

12. Your entire monthly debt load should not be more than _____% of your gross monthly income.

13. This is called your what? _____

14. The amount of house you can afford to buy depends on the terms of your mortgage and the interest rate. The term is the total length of time over which payments will be paid. This is normally _____ or _____ years.

15. What is the difference between a "fixed" rate and an "adjustable" rate? _____
_____
_____

16. Which term and rate are the most popular? (i.e. 10 years adjustable, etc.) _____
_____

17. What are some of the advantage of a 15-year term loan?

      I. _____

      II. _____

      III. _____

18. What is a disadvantage of a 15-year term loan?

      I. _____

      II. _____

      III. _____

19. What is an Adjustable Rate Mortgage (ARM)?

_____

_____

20. What are two advantages of an Adjustable Rate Mortgage (ARM)?

       I. _____

      II. _____

21. What are two disadvantages of an ARM?

       I. _____

      II. _____

22. Name three common types of mortgage loans.

       I. _____

      II. _____

     III. _____

23. This is just a regular, standard loan that does not exceed 80% of the value of the home and is either fixed nor adjustable. Your down payment is typically 20% of the purchase price of the house or market value. Which kind of loan is this: _____

24. This type of loan is only offered to veterans and it is not uncommon for them to put nothing down as a deposit. This loan guarantees part of the loan to the bank if the homeowner defaults, which makes lenders feel comfortable lending the money. Which kind of loan is this: _____

25. This loan is a partially guaranteed loan, which makes it easier for banks to give. Through this loan, the government guarantees part of your loan to the bank, so if you default, they will pay the bank back if you fail to make your payments. Which kind of loan is this: _____

26. As a first-time uneducated, misinformed home-buyer with bad credit, you are a prime candidate for becoming a victim of _____ Lending.

27. A _____ mortgage is a type of loan offered to people with very poor credit scores (often below 600).

28. What group of people are usually the target of these bad loans and mortgages?

   I. _____

   II. _____

29. What does APR Stand for? _____

30. What is an APR and how does it affect you as a homebuyer? _____
_____
_____

31. What does the Federal Truth and Lending Law require? _____
_____
_____

32. There are certain things that the APR does not include. Some of these things are:

   I. _____

   II. _____

   III. _____

   IV. _____

   V. _____

33. Why are people sometimes offered a subprime mortgage? _____
_____
_____

34. What are some clues that you may be dealing with a subprime lender?
_____
_____

35. What is the worst thing that can happen to a homeowner as a result of getting a subprime mortgage? _____

_____

36. Below, list some of the characteristics of predatory lending/subprime mortgages?

    I. _____

    II. _____

    III. _____

    IV. _____

    V. _____

37. _____ are additional up-front fees, paid in lieu of higher interest rates.

38. What is the difference between original fees and discount points? _____

_____

_____

39. Match the terms on the left with the letter of their definitions on the right:

Discount Points _____	**A.** Paid at closing to cover up the gap between the time you close and the beginning of the month.
Origination Fees _____	**B.** up-front fees, paid in lieu of higher interest rates.
Mortgage Insurance Premiums _____	**C.** Has to do with how much money you will be paying upfront in order to get the best rate for your loan.
Prepaid Mortgage Interest _____	**D.** A fee the lender charges for the work they perform on your behalf, also known as processing fees.
Annual Percentage Rate _____	**E.** Insurance that you pay against defaulting on payment of your loan.

Home Shopping

40. In searching for a home, what things should you consider about the neighborhood?

      I. _____

      II. _____

      III. _____

41. In considering a particular house or condominium (condo). What personal preferences should you consider?

      I. _____

      II. _____

      III. _____

      IV. _____

      V. _____

      VI. _____

42. Is having a Real-Estate Agent important to you? ____yes ____no

43. What are some of the things that a Real-Estate Agent does for you?

      I. _____

      II. _____

      III. _____

      IV. _____

44. What is the incentive for a Real-Estate Agent when the price of the home is high?

_____

_____

45. When are some **advantages** of having a realtor? _____

  I. _____

  II. _____

  III. _____

46. What are some **disadvantages** of having a realtor? _____

  I. _____

  II. _____

  III. _____

47. What is something else that should be seriously taken into consideration when it comes to buying a home? _____

48. Why is this important? _____

49. What happens after you make an offer to the buyer and it is agreed upon? _____
_____

50. Your deposit may be as much as _____% of the purchase price. If you pay this amount, your deposit is considered to be made.

51. With a conventional mortgage, you are expected to pay _____% of the cost of the home at closing, so although the deposit may be made, the rest of the monies are due at closing.

52. When a portion of your principle and interest payment increases slightly every month and is lowest on your first payment and highest on your last payment, it is called what? _____.

53. _____ is the largest component of your mortgage payment and offers you a huge tax break when you file your taxes.

54. On the next page, match the terms on the left with the letter of their definitions on the right:

After making an offer ____	**A.** This is an estimate of the actual value of the home by a neutral third party at the time you are trying to purchase. It helps to ensure that you are not paying too much for the home.
Paying your deposit ____	**B.** This covers insurance and taxes. Money put into this account is held by a neutral third party called an Escrow Agent who is someone from a title company or an escrow company.
Home Inspection ____	**C.** When you and your realtor determine what conditions will be in the contract, be sure to insist that the contract states that the offer is *"contingent upon a home inspection"* conducted by a qualified inspector.
Escrow ____	**D.** If you pay 5%, then your down payment is considered to be made.
Closing Day ____	**E.** The person will go through the property and perform a comprehensive visual inspection to assess the condition of the house and all of its systems.
Property Appraisal	**F.** The transfer of ownership of the house from the seller to you will officially be made and all monies owed will be paid during this time. This is the big day, the day that the house officially becomes yours!

Buying a home is a major step towards achieving the American Dream. It is a responsible step, but a very rewarding one. If you go into the process as an educated home shopper who knows what to look for, what to expect and the right questions to ask, you will have a great feeling of self-gratification and pride when you stick the keys into the door of your new home! Knowledge is key!

FINANCIAL TIPS TO REMEMBER:

- ✓ The smartest thing to do in preparation for buying your new home is to pay off as many of your bills as you can and get a copy of your Credit Report.

- ✓ Unless you shop around for a good mortgage loan, you will almost certainly pay too much in interest rates. This can cost you *tens of thousands of dollars* over the life of your loan, so choose the lowest rate and be wise.

- ✓ It is wise to get a minimum of two loan estimates and choose the one with the lowest interest rate and ideally no points.

- ✓ Good credit with high FICO scores means that you will get favorable terms on your loan. Bad credit might prevent you from getting any loan.

- ✓ Your mortgage payment should not be more than 32% of your gross monthly income. Mortgage payments normally include principal, interest, taxes and insurance also known as P.I.T.I. for short.

- ✓ Your entire monthly debt load should not be more than 40% of your gross monthly income.

- ✓ The way amortization works, the principle portion of your principle and interest payment increases slightly every month. It is lowest on your first payment and highest on your last payment.

Chapter 1 Answer Key

1. The way you handle money will eventually affect major financial purchases of your life such as:

   Your first home
   Financing a car
   Home improvements

2. Name two accounts that banks sometimes offer for no monthly fee.
   Savings
   checking

3. Name two companies that sell checkbooks at discounted prices.
   ***Checks in the Mail* (800-733-4443)**
   ***Checks Unlimited* (800-210-0468)**

4. The key to becoming wealthy is not how much money you make, but how much of it you **earn.**

5. When the amount you spend is larger than the amount you make, then the only option you have is to do what? **Cut costs and cut spending.**

6. Why is it important to save a set amount of every dollar you earn? **Answers may vary, but may include:**
   - ✓ **In order to be able to pay yourself first**
   - ✓ **So that you can have money saved in the event of an emergency**
   - ✓ **So that you can save for retirement**

7. What is the purpose of keeping a balanced checkbook? **Answers may vary, but may include: In order to be able to see what is going out and to know when your balance is getting low.**

8. List some things that can happen when your debt gets too out-of-control?
   - ✓ **Your credit will go bad**
   - ✓ **Repossessions may occur**
   - ✓ **Evictions may happen**
   - ✓ **Foreclosures may happen**
   - ✓ **Not enough money to pay bills**

9. The amount of money you bring home each month is referred to as what kind of income? **Net income**

10. Why should you check your bank account online frequently? **Answers may vary, but may include: to ensure that no illegal activity is going on, to make sure all your checks have cleared, to make sure you have enough to cover checks coming through, etc.**

11. Why should you review the amount of money you bring home each month with the amount you spend each month? **Answers may vary, but may include**

12. Why is it a good idea to check your credit report every six to twelve months?

13. Name at least seven things that you can do to keep your credit record in good standing.

    Answers may vary, but may include:

14. A budget is also called a **SPENDING** Plan.

15. What is the benefit in going AUTOMATIC? **Answers may vary, but may include:**

    - ✓ Not have to worry about sending money every month
    - ✓ You know the money is allocated without you having to think about it
    - ✓ Out of sight, out of mind
    - ✓ More convenient

16. Name some accounts that you can set up to go automatic: **Answers may vary, but may include:**

    - ✓ Emergency Fund
    - ✓ Vacation Fund
    - ✓ Savings Account
    - ✓ Retirement fund (401K, 403B, Roth)

Chapter 2 Answer Key

1. What is the benefit of sticking to a spending plan? **Answers may vary, but may include:**

    - ✓ **It helps you to stay disciplined and save**
    - ✓ **It helps you to see what you can afford and what you can't**
    - ✓ **It helps you identify what is a need and what is a want**
    - ✓ **It helps you to stay within the confines of what you can afford**

2. When creating a spending plan, what are the top five expenditures to consider?

    - ✓ **Rent/mortgage**
    - ✓ **Car payment**
    - ✓ **Utilities**
    - ✓ **Insurance**
    - ✓ **Food**
    - ✓ **Credit cards**

3. In your own words, what is an Emergency Fund?
   The emergency fund is something you put money into each month until you reach your desired goal. Financial experts recommend to save a cash reserve large enough to cover three to six month's worth of monthly expenses.

4. If you currently to not have an emergency fund, what is the first thing you should do?
   If you currently do not have an Emergency Fund or find it difficult to save, the key is to start small. Even if you only start with $10.00 in the beginning, at least you have taken the initiative to start.

5. According to what you have learned, what is the best way to get started on your Emergency Fund? **start small and make it automatic.**

6. An ideal Emergency Fund amount should have how many months of household expenses in it? **3-6 months**

7. In starting an Emergency Fund, the first thing you need to know is how much money you spend each month. On the lines below, fill in the spaces that represent your top ten monthly bills, then add them up at bottom: **Answers vary for each person.**

8. Based on the figure you have come up with, what is that amount of money that you need saved for a three month Emergency Fund? Answers vary for each person

9. How much would you need for a six-month Emergency Fund? **Answers vary for each person**

10. In order to determine if you are in debt, the first thing you should do is what? **Add up all of your monthly expenses and compare that amount with your monthly income.**

11. What typically keeps most people in debt? **Spending more than they make.**

12. Name at least two things that one should do to keep their Emergency Fund growing.

    - ✓ Make the amount automatic
    - ✓ Try not to touch the money unless it is absolutely necessary.

13. What is one of the quickest ways to accumulate debt? **Spending more than you bring in.**

14. What are some questions that you should ask yourself before you buy something that tickles your fancy, but is a non-essential. Answers may vary, but may include:

    - ✓ Are all my bills paid up?
    - ✓ Have I reached my Emergency Fund Goal?
    - ✓ Can I live without this and do I really need it?
    - ✓ What is the real reason I want it?

15. In Chapter two of your book, Money and How it Multiplies, there were 15 things listed that make your credit go bad. On the lines below, list at least ten of those 15 things listed.

    - ✓ **MAKING LATE PAYMENTS**
    - ✓ **NEGLECTING TO PAY AT ALL**
    - ✓ **LETTING AN ACCOUNT GET CHARGED OFF**
    - ✓ **LETTING AN ACCOUNT GET SENT TO COLLECTIONS**
    - ✓ **DEFAULTING ON A LOAN**
    - ✓ **FILING BANKRUPTCY**
    - ✓ **FORECLOSURE GETTING A JUDGMENT AGAINST YOU**
    - ✓ **HIGH CREDIT CARD BALANCES**
    - ✓ **MAXED OUT CREDIT CARDS**
    - ✓ **CLOSING CREDIT CARDS THAT STILL HAVE BALANCES**
    - ✓ **CLOSING OLD CREDIT CARDS**
    - ✓ **APPLYING FOR SEVERAL CREDIT CARDS OR LOANS**
    - ✓ **HAVING ONLY CREDIT CARDS OR ONLY LOANS**
    - ✓ **CO-SIGNING FOR SOMEONE**

Chapter 3 Answer Key

1. Based upon what you have learned, what is credit? **Credit is receiving something without fully paying for it at the time that you get it.**

2. What is the main factor for a lender to determine your ability to pay back a loan? **Your income is a main factor indicating whether or not you will be able to pay back the loan.**

3. Name two other factors that a creditor will consider before giving you a loan?
   - ✓ **Your income is a main factor indicating whether or not you will be able to pay back the loan.**
   - ✓ **The amount of debt you already have is another main factor taken into account.**
   - ✓ **The amount of borrowing that you have already done and how well you made those payments is another indicator of your intention and ability to pay back what you are seeking to borrow.**

4. In your own words, what is an Annual Percentage Rate? Answers may vary, but may include:
   The APR usually appears in the "terms" section of the Credit Application and takes into account how long it will take you to pay back the loan.

5. What is the first thing a lender looks at when you apply for credit?
   Your Credit Report is the first thing that lenders look at when you apply for a credit card or want to make a major purchase.

6. In your own words, what is a Credit Report? **Your Credit Report is a detailed record of your payment history with lenders and is an indicator that reflects how well or badly you manage your financial matters.**

7. Your Credit Report is maintained by companies called what? **Credit Bureaus**

8. What is the role of lenders after they extend credit to you regarding your payment history? **After approving you, the lender/creditor submits information regarding your paying strength to the credit bureaus.**

9. What kinds of information do lenders report after they extend credit to you? **How much you borrowed, how much you have paid back so far, your credit limit, the type of account you have, date the account was opened and whether the account has been delinquent.**

10. Name some public financial records that may also appear on your credit report? **Accounts that have been sent to collections, Public records such as bankruptcies, tax liens, foreclosures, or lawsuit judgments appear on your Credit Report too.**

11. What is some personal information that does not appear on your credit report? **Personal information like your name, current and previous addresses and current and previous employers also appear**

on your Credit Report, but not your race, marital status, religious beliefs, political affiliation, savings or checking account information, and/or any arrest records.

12. What is a credit bureau? **A credit bureau is an agency that gathers information on how consumers use their credit and how they pay back what they borrowed.**

13. Name the three top credit bureaus in the United States: **Experian, TransUnion, and Equifax**

14. Why is your credit score important?
Credit reporting makes it possible for stores to accept your checks, for banks to issue credit or debit cards to you and for corporations to manage their operations. Depending on your credit score, lenders will determine what risk you pose to them.

15. If your credit score is bad, a lender may still extend credit to you, but what is the downside to this? **They will lend you money at a higher annual percentage rate verses someone with a better credit score.**

16. What ultimately makes the difference in the monthly payment? **The difference in interest includes a large impact on the monthly payments, which includes both interest and principal.**

17. What is a F.I.C.O. Score? **A FICO (Fair Isaac Corporation) Score is calculated based on the information contained in your Credit Report. The numbers are generated by a computer program that runs through your Report.**

18. What is the benefit in having a high FICO (credit) score: **The higher your credit score, the better loan and interest rates you will qualify for.**

19. A FICO score takes into account a lot of different information from your Credit Report, but it is not all weighted equally. Name the five areas and percentages that make up a FICO score.

- ✓ **Payment History – 35%**
- ✓ **Total Amounts Owed – 30%**
- ✓ **Length of Credit History – 15%**
- ✓ **New Credit – 10%**
- ✓ **Type of Credit in Use – 10%**

20. Notes left on your credit reports are usually indicated by codes indicated by **R1 to R9**. The "R" means that it is a "revolving" account. An R1 means that the account is a revolving account in good standing. An R9 means a revolving account in very poor standing. R1s and R9s are two extremes of the many account classifications that your creditors can add to your Credit Report. In the box below, complete the table with the appropriate R score.

R	REVOLVING
0	Little or no credit history
1	Paid as agreed
2	30+ days past due
3	60+ days past due
4	90+ days past due
5	120+ days past the due date
6	This rating does not exist
7	Making regular payments under wage earner plan (popular name for a debt repayment plan under Chapter 13 of the Bankruptcy Code.)
8	Repossession
9	Charge off to bad debt

21. On the average, how long does derogatory information remain on your credit report? **7 years**

22. How often should you check your credit report? **2 times a year**

23. What is the best method of obtaining a copy of your credit report? **The best method of obtaining your Credit Report is to send a written request. Make sure that you ask for your credit score as well (not just the report) because the Credit Report and the credit score are two different things.**

24. What is an alternate way of obtaining your credit report? **You can also request a copy online at www.annualcreditreport.com.**

25. What are some ways in which you may obtain a free copy of your credit report? **If your application for credit is denied, you are entitled to a free Credit Report.**

Chapter 4 Answer Key

1. What is the difference between a credit card and a debit card? **A debit card is equivalent to using cash because the money comes directly out of your checking account. The card should decline if the money is not in your account, although it does sometimes approve. However, you do not pay interest on the items you buy when you use your debit card, but when you use your credit card, there is interest added on to the principal balance.**

2. What are some of the benefits in having a credit card? **A credit card is a great financial backup and having the credit available for emergencies is definitely a life-saver, but your credit card should only be used for emergencies.**

3. What are some good books to read on financing and money management? Answers may vary, but may include:

    Smart Women Finish Rich (David Bach);
    Rich Dad Poor Dad (Robert Kiyosaki);
    Richest man in Babylon (George S. Clason);
    The Automatic Millionaire (David Bach);
    The Millionaire Next Door (Thomas Stanley and William Danko).

4. What is Emotional Spending?
    When people shop to make them feel better. Some people resort to this when they are feeling depressed, have anxiety, are frustrated, stressed, bored, feel under-appreciated, are feeling inferior, etc.

5. Why should you never buy anything when you are desperate for it? **Because you will end up paying too much money for it and/or buy something you really are not crazy about. The bottom line is that you should always be level-headed when you shop.**

6. Are there some things that you purchase once a day, once a week, or once a month? If so list them and complete the activity below. **Answers will vary for A-E**

7. When a consumer borrows money from a bank so that they can make a big purchase such as a house, car, or boat etc, that is called what? **Financing**

8. Once a bank approves a loan that you have applied for, what do they do next? **The bank will pay the merchant the total cost for what you are buying and they (the bank) will send you a bill each month.**

9. If you find that you are wasting a lot of money, would you be willing to curtail your spending? ___ yes ___ no. Why or why not? **Answers will vary**

TRUE OR FALSE?

10. It is fine to use credit cards for food and toiletries. **FALSE**

11. All credit cards have the same Annual Percentage Rate. **FALSE**

12. A credit card should ideally be used for emergency purposes only. **Can be true or false**

13. All credit cards have an annual fee. **FALSE**

14. Credit cards and debit cards are basically the same thing. **FALSE**

15. One should wait until they get older to save for retirement. **FALSE**

16. There are advantages and disadvantages to having credit cards. On the lines below list **three advantages** to having credit cards. **Answers may vary, but should include three of the following:**

    - ✓ **Able to get essential items right away if you do not have the available cash**
    - ✓ **No need to carry cash**
    - ✓ **Creates a record of purchases**
    - ✓ **Easier than writing checks**
    - ✓ **Improves your credit every time you make an on-time minimum payment**

17. On the lines list **three disadvantages** to having credit cards. **Answers may vary, but should include three of the following:**

    - ✓ **You pay interest on everything you buy**
    - ✓ **May pay additional fees, including annual fees**
    - ✓ **The available credit may increase the impulse to buy things you do not really need**
    - ✓ **When you open a new credit card account, you make an impact on your credit score, reducing 5 points from the fico score with each new card**

18. On the lines below, list some of your **Credit Card Responsibilities** as a credit card holder. **Answers may vary, but should include three of the following:**

    - ✓ **Spend only what you can repay**
    - ✓ **Read and understand your credit card contract**
    - ✓ **Pay at least the minimum amount due on time**
    - ✓ **Know your interest rates**
    - ✓ **Notify your creditor if you cannot meet payments**
    - ✓ **Report lost or stolen credit cards immediately**
    - ✓ **Never give your card number over the phone unless you initiated the call or are certain of the caller's identity**
    - ✓ **Get a credit card with the lowest interest rate possible and no annual fees**
    - ✓ **Read the fine print located on the back of your billing statement and yearly disclosure statement.**

19. On the lines below, list some facts that you have learned about credit cards.

- **Bank of America, J.P. Morgan, Chase, Citigroup, Capital One, Discover, and American Express. They account for about 90% of all credit card debt.**
- **As of 2007, 78% of all American households had credit cards and 60% of these households carried a balance.**
- **Statistics show that 78% of college students had at least one credit card. Nearly 40% of Freshman students sign-up for credit cards and almost 20% get them in high school.**
- **Of the 78% who have credit cards, 32% have 4 or more cards**
- **It would take roughly 12 years for a student to pay off a $1,000 credit card debt with an 18% interest rate if they are only making minimum payments.**
- **Banks that specialize in credit cards have been much more profitable than banks in general. According to FDIC data for 2007, the return on equity was 15.1% for credit card banks, compared to 8.2% for all banks.**
- **Credit card companies collected $115 billion in revenue in 2006, about two-thirds from interest payments, one-fifth from fees paid by merchants who accept the cards, and about 15% from consumer fees.**
- **When you are attempting to pay off credit card debt, always pay the credit card with the highest rate of interest first**

20. What are the main components of the Credit Card Accountability, Responsibility and Disclosure Act of 2009?
    - **MUST HAVE A NOTE FROM YOUR PARENTS**
    - **NO MORE FREE GIVEAWAYS FOR FILLING OUT AN APPLICATION**
    - **NO MORE SECRET DEALS**
    - **NO RELEASE OF CREDIT REPORTS FOR STUDENTS UNDER AGE 21**
    - **NO MORE OVER-THE-LIMIT FEES**
    - **LATE FEES CAPPED**

21. What is bankruptcy? Bankruptcy is an option that is considered when the debt of a person, company or organization becomes too much to pay.

22. Most cases of bankruptcy are filed under what three codes?
    - *Chapter 7*
    - *Chapter 13*
    - *Chapter 11*

23. This code is a formal declaration that you are willingly working with creditors so that they will get their money, but at a slightly slower rate than they might have wanted. By promising to pay off your debts, you are allowed to keep valuable personal items rather than turning them over to be sold. **CHAPTER 13**

24. Under this code, filing means that the business intends to continue operating while the bankruptcy court supervises the company's debt and contractual obligations. The court has the power to cancel all or some

of the company's debts. The company can then make a fresh start without having the financial burden hanging over their head. **CHAPTER 11**

25. This filing means the selling off of your valuable assets in order to pay your debts. It does not mean that all of your debt is eliminated entirely. It means that all "unsecured" debt does not have to be paid back, but the "secured" debt must be dealt with in some kind of way. **CHAPTER 7**

26. How does filing bankruptcy affect your credit?
Your credit rating will be devastated by any kind of bankruptcy, but a chapter 13 looks a little better on your credit record than a 7. When you file for a bankruptcy, you are saying to the world that you are no longer worthy to be trusted with future credit and with a bankruptcy on your Credit Report

Chapter 5 Answer Key

1. What is the benefit of setting financial goals and making plans for your financial future? **Answers may vary, but may include:**

   - **You have a clear focus of what you want to achieve and how much it will take to achieve it**
   - **You are less inclined to purchase non essentials with a goal in mind.**
   - **You can keep track of your progress and how soon the goal with be achieved.**
   - **You take control of your life. Setting goals is a vital step towards improving your financial independence.**

2. What are the two main things that determine the amount of federal income tax you pay?

   - **Your filing status**
   - **How many exemptions you claim on your w4 form**

3. For the current year, what percentage of your paycheck goes to FICA (Federal Insurance Contribution Act)? **Answers may vary based upon the current year.**

4. For the current year, what percentage of your paycheck goes to Medicare? **Answers may vary based upon the current year.**

5. The amount of money you have left after all of your deductions have been taken out is called your what? **Net income**

6. What percentage of your income should you use to PAY YOURSELF FIRST? **Typically 10%**

7. What two accounts should you regularly put money into with the 10% that you use to pay yourself first? **Answers may vary but should include one of the following**

   - **Retirement**
   - **Emergency fund**

8. What is the purpose of the first account (above)? To begin saving for retirement. **The younger you start, the more financially secure you will be when you are ready to retire.**

9. What is the purpose of the second account (above)? **In case an emergency arises that requires immediate attention such as: tires for the car, a hot water heater, the AC goes out, the refrigerator breaks down, funeral expenses, etc.**

10. Once you secure your career, what is the first thing you should do?
Inquire about the retirement benefits and start your retirement fund as soon as possible.

11. What is the purpose of a Retirement Plan? **To decide now how you will live after you have stopped working.**

12. What is the best way to put money into these accounts without having to think about doing it every time you get paid? **Having it automatically deducted from your paycheck. In other words, going automatic!**

13. What is the benefit in starting to save for retirement while you are young? **The younger you are when you start, the wealthier you will become. How you may ask? Because of the POWER OF COMPOUNDING!**

14. What does "tax deferred" mean? **It means that the salary deferrals are pre-taxed until you reach the age of being able to withdraw it.**

15. When your retirement plan does not allow you to invest in stocks, but give options of annuities, mutual funds and money market funds to invest in, this is which plan? **403B Plan**

16. When your employer-sponsored retirement plan includes publicly traded securities and mutual funds, this is usually which plan? **401K**

17. With the Roth IRA, what is the maximum amount of money that can be contributed to the account each year? **5,000 for those under 50 years old.**

18. A person over 50 may contribute up to how much into their IRA? **6,000 as year.**

19. What is the age that you can make a withdrawal out of your retirement accounts without penalty? **59 ½**

20. At what age can you open an Roth IRA? **Any age**

21. Name two popular Retirement Plans that companies, organizations, or businesses offer to their employees. **401K & 403B**

22. What is an incentive that some organizations do for their employees when they contribute to their Retirement Plan? **Some companies match the amount of money that employees put into their account.**

23. If you leave a company that offered a Retirement Plan and begin working at a company that does not offer the plan, what can you do with the money you contributed from your previous employer? **You can do what is called a 401k rollover to your new company if the new company offers 401Ks or 403Bs.**

24. Look at the IRA characteristics below and put a **"R"** if the statement belongs to a Roth IRA and put a **"T"** if the statement refers to a Traditional IRA.

R	Individuals of all ages can open up a Roth
T	Pay a 10% penalty for early withdrawal
T	Must be at least 18 to open up a retirement account
T	You have to withdraw a minimum amount
T	Pay no taxes when you withdraw money at age 59 ½
T	Assets can be passed onto beneficiaries after death.
R	Contributions can be withdrawn at any time, tax free.
R	There are no required minimum distributions
T	Pay taxes on the money you withdraw
T	Contributions ARE tax deductible
R	Contributions are NOT tax deductible

25. When the money you make from an initial investment is reinvested to make even more money than the initial investment that is called what? **compounding**

Chapter 6 Answer Key

1. The biggest tax you pay to the government is what? **Federal withholding**

2. What is the name of the form that determines how much money will be taken out of your check when you are hired at a job? **W4**

3. How often does the company you work for pay the federal withholding taxes to the government? **Every quarter (3 months).**

4. How do the more dependants you claim on your W4 form affect the money that you bring home? **The more dependants you claim on you w4, the more money you bring home.**

5. How do the less dependants you claim on your W4 form affect the money that you bring home? **The less number of dependants you claim on you w4, the less money you bring home.**

6. Why do some people have their federal withholding percentage set high? Answers may vary, but may include the following:
   - **So they can get a bigger refund during tax season**
   - **To offset the amount in taxes that they will have to pay during tax season**

7. What is FICA *(Federal Insurance Contributions Act)*? **FICA is a percentage of money that is taken out of the paychecks of working individuals to pay Social Security Retirement and Medicare (Hospital Insurance) benefits to older Americans. It is a mandatory payroll deduction for every working individual.**

8. What kinds of things does FICA pay for? **FICA tax deductions also provide benefits to widows and widowers, children who have lost their working parents, and disabled workers who qualify for benefits.**

9. What does FICA tax pay when it is deducted from your paycheck? **Same as above**

10. What is the percentage of FICA that is taken out of everyone's paycheck? **7.65%**

11. Broken down, what is the individual percentage of social security and Medicare that makes the total FICA tax?

    SS: **6.2%**

    Medicare **1.45%**

12. Your tax bracket depends upon two things: 1.) your taxable income and 2.) your filing status. What are the codes for the following tax brackets (1-5)?

    Single **1**
    Married Filing Jointly **2**
    Married Filing Separately **3**
    Head of Household **4**
    Qualifying Widow(er) **5**

13. How many years should a person retain copies of their tax returns? **At least 7 years**

14. Do you have medical insurance? ___yes ___ no **Answers will vary.**

15. If not, what will you do if you require medical attention? **Answers will vary.**

16. How do you plan on getting medical insurance in the near future if you do not have any? **Answers will vary.**

17. Do you have life insurance? ___yes ___ no **Answers will vary.**

    If yes, do you know which of the two kinds it is (term or whole life)?
    ___yes ___ no

18. What is the difference between the two different kinds of life insurance? **The main difference between the two is the period of time that the insurance policy is valid, either for a short "term" or for your "whole" life.**

19. Analyzing your personal situation, which type of insurance is best for you? **Answers will vary.**

20. Do you have enough life insurance to bury you and pay off all your debt? ___yes ___ no **Answers will vary.**

PART B:

24. If you have credit cards, complete the exercises below. If not, skip the exercise.

    List all your credit cards on the next page:

    Answers will vary.

25. Based on the table above, how much money do you owe in credit card debt? **Answers will vary.**

    In helping you to develop a Spending Plan, complete the following exercises:

26. My annual (gross) income is: _____   My net income (every paycheck) is _____. My federal withholding amount is _____. My FICA/Social Security amount is _____. **Answers will vary.**

List all of your payroll deductions and amounts below: **Answers will vary.**

DEDUCTION	AMOUNT	TOTAL
Ex: Medical Ins.	$ 153.00	$153.00
United Way	$15.00	$168.00

27. According to your figures above, what is the total amount of your deductions including taxes?

Answers will vary.

28. Review all of your deductions above and see if there are any that you can cut out. List them below:

Answers will vary.

On the lines below, make a list all of your household expenses.

Example:	AMOUNT	TOTAL
Rent	$650.00	$650.00
Car Payment	$300.00	$950.00

29. My total monthly expenses are: **Answers will vary.**

30. As I review my income and calculate my monthly expenses, I am (choose one): **Answers will vary.**

___ in the green (positive) with _____ dollars left over each month.

___ in the red (negative) by _____ dollars each month.

31. If you have money left over each month, do you see where the extra money (surplus) goes? **Answers will vary.**

(The exercise on page 32 can help reveal where the money goes.)

32. If you do not have money left over, what do you need to do to change this? **Answers will vary.**

33. Based on what you have learned, where should your extra money be going? **Answers will vary.**

Part C: FINANCIAL EXERCISE:
For one month, keep a record of everything you spend. Do this for 30 consecutive days. If you start on April 15th, then you must review your findings on May 15th. This includes everything paid out of your net income (rent, car payment, utilities, clothes, food, etc.) This does not include deductions that are already taken out.

Date to begin: Answers will vary.

You are given extra lines for the days that you buy more than one or two things in a day. (You may buy a new shirt, then gas, then a meal at Red Lobster. You may then pick up a prescription at the local drug store – all in the same day. You must keep track of each of these things and put them in your log.

DATE	STORE	PURCHASE	AMOUNT	TOTAL

After making an offer **C**	**A.** This is an estimate of the actual value of the home by a neutral third party at the time you are trying to purchase. It helps to ensure that you are not paying too much for the home.
Paying your deposit **D**	**B.** This covers insurance and taxes. Money put into this account is held by a neutral third party called an Escrow Agent who is someone from a title company or an escrow company.
Home Inspection **E**	**C.** When you and your realtor determine what conditions will be in the contract, be sure to insist that the contract states that the offer is *"contingent upon a home inspection"* conducted by a qualified inspector.
Escrow **B**	**D.** If you pay 5%, then your down payment is considered to be made.
Closing Day **F**	**E.** The person will go through the property and perform a comprehensive visual exam to assess the condition of the house and all of its systems.
Property Appraisal **A**	**F.** The transfer of ownership of the house from the seller to you will officially be made and all monies owed will be paid during this time. This is the big day, the day that the house officially becomes yours!

Chapter 7 Answer Key

1. What are some of the differences between home ownership and renting? **Answers may vary but may include:**

    i. **You don't pay for a lot of the repairs when you rent.**
    ii. **As a homeowner, you have to pay for all of the repairs.**
    iii. **As a homeowner, you must pay taxes and insurance on your home.**

2. How soon in advance should you typically begin preparing for homeownership? **At least one year.**

3. What are the main three things that should be done BEFORE you begin the home-buying process?

    i. **Save money for the down payment and the upfront costs**
    ii. **Pay off as many of your bills as possible**
    iii. **Review your credit report and correct as many errors as possible.**

4. What is the difference between getting pre-qualified and getting pre-approved? **A prequalification is optional, but a preapproval is mandatory.**

5. During the pre-approval process, you will need certain documents. List some of the documents that you will need when seeking to apply for a home loan. **Answers will vary, but must include some of the following:**

    - Your last four paycheck stubs
    - Six months worth of bank statements from all bank accounts you have
    - Three years worth of tax returns
    - Proof of any additional income (child support, etc)
    - Proof of how you will make the down payment
    - Written explanations for any late payments you may have on your Credit Report
    - Written explanations for any charge offs, repossessions, evictions or other derogatory entries on your credit report.

6. What is the primary thing that creditors look for when a client seeks to apply for a home loan? **How much money your make and your credit report.**

7. How soon after a client applies for a home loan should they receive the Good Faith Estimate?

Within 3 business days of applying for a home loan.

8. What is a GFE? **It is a standard form which is intended to be used to compare different offers from different lenders or brokers. It includes an itemized list of fees and costs associated with your loan estimate.**

9. Why should you carefully review the GFE when you get it? **Because the lender directly controls many of the fees on it, and those are the ones that you must pay the most attention to when comparing loan offers.**

10. Your mortgage payment should not be more than **32%** of your gross monthly income?

11. This is known as your what? **This figure is known as your Gross Debt Service (GDS) ratio.**

12. Your entire monthly debt load should not be more than **40%** of your gross monthly income.

13. This is called your what? **This figure is called your Total Debt Service (TDS) ratio.**

14. The amount of house you can afford to buy depends on the terms of your mortgage and the interest rate. The term is the total length of time over which payments will be paid. This is normally **15 or 30 years.**

15. What is the difference between a "fixed" rate and an "adjustable" rate? **A fixed rate is a mortgage in which the interest rate does not change during the entire life of the loan. An Adjustable Rate Mortgage (ARM) has an interest rate that is fixed for the first several years of the loan (typically 3, 5, or 7 years) then goes up or down for the remainder of the loan based on market conditions.**

16. Which term and rate are the most popular? (i.e. 10 years adjustable, etc.) **30 year fixed, (15 year is common also, but 30 is the most common.)**

17. What are some of the advantage of a 15-year term loan? **A 15-year term lowers your interest rate, reduces total interest payments and increases principal payments.**

18. What is a disadvantage of a 15-year term loan? **Your monthly payment is higher**

19. What is an Adjustable Rate Mortgage (ARM)? **Adjustable-rate Mortgages offer initial rates that are lower than fixed mortgages. At some point, however, usually after the first year, the rates are tied to market conditions and are subject to rate increases.**

20. What are two advantages of an Adjustable Rate Mortgage (ARM)? **Some ARMs offer initial rates at least 2% below fixed rates and limit increases to 1%**

21. What are two disadvantages of an ARM? **You must have the money to be able to afford the monthly payment when it increases and sometimes it increases double or even triple what you are used to paying.**

22. Name three common types of mortgage loans.
    - *Conventional*
    - *Federal Housing Association (FHA).*
    - *Veteran Affairs Loans (VA).*

23. This is just a regular, standard loan that does not exceed 80% of the value of the home and is either fixed nor adjustable. Your down payment is typically 20% of the purchase price of the house or market value. Which kind of loan is this: *Conventional*

24. This type of loan is only offered to veterans and it is not uncommon for them to put nothing down as a deposit. This loan guarantees part of the loan to the bank if the homeowner defaults, which makes lenders feel comfortable lending the money. Which kind of loan is this: *Veteran Affairs Loans (VA).*

25. This loan is a partially guaranteed loan, which makes it easier for banks to give. Through this loan, the government guarantees part of your loan to the bank, so if you default, they will pay the bank back if you fail to make your payments. Which kind of loan is this: *Federal Housing Association (FHA).*

26. As a first-time uneducated, misinformed home-buyer with bad credit, you are a prime candidate for becoming a victim of Lending. **Predatory lending**

27. A mortgage is a type of loan offered to people with very poor credit scores (often below 600) **Subprime mortgage**

28. What group of people are usually the target of these bad loans and mortgages?

    - **the elderly**
    - **the economically disadvantaged (those who live in low-income neighborhoods)**
    - **African American neighborhoods**

29. What does APR Stand for? **Annual Percentage Rate**

30. What is an APR and how does it affect you as a homebuyer? APR stands for **It has to do with how much money you will be paying upfront in order to get the best rate for your loan. It is nothing more than an *estimate* of the various costs of your loan, including the interest rate.**

31. What does the Federal Truth and Lending Law require? **The *Federal Truth in Lending Law* requires mortgage companies to list the APR of their loans when they advertise an interest rate. This prevents them from advertising unduly low interest rates and then tacking on fees and other costs that drive up the real cost of the loan.**

32. There are certain things that the APR does not include. Some of these things are:

- *Discount Points*
- *Origination Fees*
- *Mortgage Insurance Premiums*
- *Prepaid Mortgage Interest*

33. Why are people sometimes offered a subprime mortgage? **Because their credit score is so low that no one else will give them a conventional mortgage.**

34. What are some clues that you may be dealing with a subprime lender?

35. What is the worst thing that can happen to a homeowner as a result of getting a subprime mortgage?

36. Below, list some of the characteristics of predatory lending/subprime mortgages?

Excessive Fees:
Prepayment Penalty
Tax Refund Anticipation Loans (RALs)
Insurance and Other Unnecessary Products:
Abusive and Abnormal Prepayment Penalties:
Loan Flipping:
Mandatory Arbitration:

37. What are additional up-front fees, paid in lieu of higher interest rates. *Discount Points* **Discount Points are additional up-front fees, paid in lieu of higher interest rates. When your money is low, lenders usually charge points, also known as Loan Origination Fees. Each "point" is equal to 1 percent of the loan amount. Therefore, 2 points on a $100,000 loan will cost $2,000. The higher the cost of the home, the more expensive the points are.**

38. What is the difference between original fees and discount points?
This is a fee the lender charges for the work they perform on your behalf, also known as processing fees. Basically, it is the same as the labor that you pay when someone works on your car.

39. Match the terms on the left with the letter of their definitions on the right:

Discount Points **B**	**A.** Paid at closing to cover up the gap between the time you close and the beginning of the month.
Origination Fees **D**	**B.** up-front fees, paid in lieu of higher interest rates.
Mortgage Insurance Premiums **E**	**C.** Has to do with how much money you will be paying upfront in order to get the best rate for your loan.
Prepaid Mortgage Interest **A**	**D.** A fee the lender charges for the work they perform on your behalf, also known as processing fees.
Annual Percentage Rate **B**	**E.** Insurance that you pay against defaulting on payment of your loan.

40. In searching for a home, what things should you consider about the neighborhood?

41. In considering a particular house or condominium (condo). What personal preferences should you consider?

42. Is having a Real-Estate Agent important to you? ____yes ____no

43. What are some of the things that a Real-Estate Agent does for you?

44. What is the incentive for a Real-Estate Agent when the price of the home is high?

45. When are some **advantages** of having a realtor?

46. What are some **disadvantages** of having a realtor?
47. What is something else that should be seriously taken into consideration when it comes to buying a home?

48. Why is this important?

49. What happens after you make an offer to the buyer and it is agreed upon? **A contract is drawn up.**

50. Your deposit may be as much as **20%** of the purchase price. If you pay this amount, your deposit is considered to be made.

51. With a conventional mortgage, you are expected to pay **20%** of the cost of the home at closing, so although the deposit may be made, the rest of the monies are due at closing.

52. When a portion of your principle and interest payment increases slightly every month and is lowest on your first payment and highest on your last payment, it is called what? Adjustable rate mortgage

53. **Interest** is the largest component of your mortgage payment and offers you a huge tax break when you file your taxes.

54. Match the terms below on the left with the letter of their definitions on the right:

After making an offer **C**	**A.** This is an estimate of the actual value of the home by a neutral third party at the time you are trying to purchase. It helps to ensure that you are not paying too much for the home.
Paying your deposit **D**	**B.** This covers insurance and taxes. Money put into this account is held by a neutral third party called an Escrow Agent who is someone *from* a title company or an escrow company.
Home Inspection **E**	**C.** When you and your realtor determine what conditions will be in the contract, be sure to insist that the contract states that the offer is *"contingent upon a home inspection"* conducted by a qualified inspector.
Escrow **B**	**D.** If you pay 5%, then your down payment is considered to be made.
Closing Day **F**	**E.** The person will go through the property and perform a comprehensive visual exam to assess the condition of the house and all of its systems.
Property Appraisal **A**	**F.** The transfer of ownership of the house from the seller to you will officially be made and all monies owed will be paid during this time. This is the big day, the day that the house officially becomes yours!

Dr. Mia Y. Merritt

www.miamerritt.com
merrittmia@yahoo.com
1-866-560-7652

Dr. Mia Y. Merritt was born, raised and currently resides in Miami Florida. She received her education in the Miami-Dade County Public School System and served as an educator for over 18 years. Her experience as a teacher, Assistant Principal, College Professor and mentor has afforded her the experience to work with youth and adults of all ages. She is a Certified Keynote Speaker, Teen/Youth Facilitator, Prosperity Coach and Author.

Dr. Merritt provides keynotes speeches, workshops, seminars and keynote speeches around the country to organizations such as the U.S. Department of Homeland Security, The Miami-Dade County City Mangers, Florida International University, The University of Miami, Florida Memorial University, Family Christian Association and many more.

She is also a Minister of the Gospel and is a member of Peace Missionary Baptist Church in Miami, Florida under the leadership of Rev. Dr. Tracy McCloud. Dr. Merritt is the recipient of the 2011 African American Achiever's Award sponsored by JM Family Enterprises and has received other awards and accolades for her accomplishments.

She holds a Bachelors Degree in Elementary Education, a Masters Degree in Exceptional Education, a Specialist Degree in Educational Leadership and a Doctorate Degree in Organizational Leadership.

Dr. Merritt is a published author of twelve books on the subjects of spirituality, personal development, prosperity, self-empowerment, and adult education. Dr. Merritt's challenges and experiences in life have produced in her the resilience, character and strength to persevere in spite of what challenges she faces. She shares her experiences in an impactful way in order to inspire, encourage and remind others that their past does not dictate their future.

www.ingramcontent.com/pod-product-compliance
Lightning Source LLC
Chambersburg PA
CBHW081259170426
43198CB00017B/2847